MW00936515

Alexander Kennedy

Amazon.com/author/alexanderkennedy

Contents

Prologue

An architect, a microbiologist, and an astronomer walk into a bar. This was the set-up not for a bad joke, but for one of the most consequential meetings in scientific history. The year was 1684, and it was shortly after a meeting of The President, Council, and Fellows of the Royal Society of London for Improving Natural Knowledge—usually just known as the Royal Society.

The venue was actually only half-bar, and half what we today would call a coffee shop, a type of establishment just coming into vogue across Europe. The first coffee shop in Paris had opened only ten years before, and another four decades would pass before one appeared in Berlin. But they had reached London in the 1650s, and had multiplied by the hundreds. As historian Timothy Blanning has observed, coffee houses had already made themselves into a special kind of space, a public space for the free exchange of ideas, where young men (and much more rarely, women) could rail against the politicians of their day or debate new conceptions of the arts of sciences. Nor is it a coincidence that they were associated with what a later generation would call Enlightenment ideals and scientific progress; whereas the previous social drink of choice, ale, tended to deaden one's faculties, coffee stimulated them and spurred them on.

The three men who now sat around the table, all Royal fellows, had in mind just such a scientific exchange as they drank from their steaming bowls of black coffee.

The first of the trio was Christopher Wren, already one of the most famous architects of English history. Wren's great chance had come with the Great Fire of London in 1666, which had consumed more than 13,000 houses, necessitating massive reconstruction. Wren had rebuilt 52 of London's churches after the blaze, including St. Paul's Cathedral, and had designed a monument to the victims of the fire itself. Like many great men of his age, Wren was something of a polymath—with so many sciences in their infancy, it was possible for an educated man to make discoveries in any number of fields. With his interests in mathematics and physics, he had helped found the Royal Society, and had stepped down as president only two years before.

The second of the trio was Robert Hooke, one of the least likeable geniuses science would produce until James Watson. Hooke was irascible, boastful, jealous, and all-around nasty, determined to crush any scientific competitor, even at the cost of impeding the progress of human knowledge. But others tolerated him because of his legitimate genius. Hooke had been an assistant to the early chemist Robert Boyle, and aided in the experiments that resulted in Boyle's gas law; in his own right, he had pioneered the use of the microscope to observe living tissue, and was the one who gave "cells" their name, as well as working on refraction. An account of his appearance written around this time described him as of "midling stature, something crooked, pale faced, and his face but little below, but his head is lardge, his eie full and popping, and not quick; a grey eie. He haz a delicate head of haire, browne, and of an excellent moist curle."

We can imagine that full, grey, popping eye fixed on the third man at the table, Edmond Halley, as he sipped his coffee. Halley was handsome, tall, and kind where Hooke was crooked, cranky, and repulsive, and was without question the junior member of this trio. When Wren and Hooke had been doing important surveying and rebuilding after the 1666 Great Fire, Halley had been only five years old. Halley would not compute the path of the comet that now bears his name until 1705. At the time of this fateful meeting, his sole claim to fame (and ticket into the Royal Society) was an extensive star chart he had made for the Southern Hemisphere while stationed at Saint Helena—the same island where Napoleon Bonaparte would be imprisoned more than a century later.

The men's conversation likely ranged over many scientific controversies of their day. Perhaps they discussed the nature of sound, or the debate over whether light was a wave (as Rene Descartes and Christaan Huygens argued) or a particle, as another Royal fellow, Isaac Newton, believed he had demonstrated (see Chapter 4). But eventually, their conversation settled on gravity. Halley posed Wren and Hooke an important question: if the planets were attracted to the sun by an invisible force, and this force was inversely proportional to distance, what shape would the resulting orbits have?

Halley was likely proud of his sophisticated question to his betters, the result of months of painstaking calculations. But to his surprise, both men responded with laughter. Hooke explained that this hypothesis had been tried by many before, but actually proving it was the difficulty. Wren agreed, stating that he had tested the hypothesis but had never been able to prove it. Hooke claimed, in typical fashion, that he had written such a proof long ago but kept it to himself. Halley may have been the youngest man at the table, but he was not stupid, and he called out Hooke's story as the obvious nonsense that it was.

Wren cut off the budding argument with a formal wager. He would give Hooke and Halley two months. The first man to prove the inverse-squares hypothesis would receive a forty-shilling book as a gift. Two months quickly passed. Halley made no progress, despite his best efforts. Hooke cheekily continued to claim to know the secret, but refused to share it. Now Wren, too, was prepared to openly call Hooke a liar.

Halley had lost the wager, but he was increasingly obsessed with the problem. He had heard of a Cambridge professor of mathematics, primarily known for his work in optics but said to have an interest in physical mechanics. Halley had met him briefly once before, but surely he approached the meeting with trepidation, as the professor had a reputation for aloofness and an irritability that nearly matched Hooke's. Still, Halley pressed on. He traveled to Cambridge and called on Newton without warning, determined not to let the older man avoid the meeting.

We know that Halley did not pose his fateful query right away; they talked for some time first, though of what is lost to history. But when Halley did finally share the reason for his visit—the inverse-squares conjecture—Newton had a ready answer. The resulting orbit would be an ellipse. Since the planets' orbits were now known to be elliptical, this was exactly what Halley had been hoping to hear.

He pressed Newton for the proof, but Newton had apparently mislaid it. After some searching, Newton asked his visitor if he could send the proof later. Halley agreed, returned to London, and began a long wait. For three months, he watched the mail. At times, he must have suspected that it was Hooke all over again—but Newton, unlike Hooke, was as good as his word. He finally sent Halley De Motu Corporum Gyrum ("On the Motion of Revolving Bodies"), a nine-page proof of the inverse-squares conjecture.

Hooke had been right about one thing. To prove this conjecture was to prove everything about cosmic motion. Here Newton not only demonstrated in elegant mathematics why the planets moved in elliptical orbits, but how any object would behave while moving through a gravitational field. Suddenly the heavens fitted together in a way they never had before. Halley had chronicled their movements one star at a time, arc second by arc second, day by day. Newton had found the laws that made all the stars move, and he had summed them up in nine pages.

Halley was both stunned and overjoyed. In response to this pamphlet, Halley made the greatest scientific contribution of his life. He set his own ego and career aside—something neither Hooke nor even Wren could have done in a similar spot—and dedicated himself to furthering Newton's work instead. He coaxed this delicate, temperamental man through years of labor, persuading him to again risk public conflict by sending his findings to the Royal Society. Two years after writing De Motu

Corporum Gyrum, Newton finished and submitted his masterpiece, probably the most important work in scientific history: Philosophiæ Naturalis Principia Mathematica ("Principles of Natural Philosophy"). In the words of biographer David Berlinski, it was "a work that stands to his earlier treatise as an oak to an acorn."

The Principia contained Newton's three laws of motion (see Chapter 6) and his groundbreaking work on gravity (see Chapter 7). Most importantly, it built these laws into a system by which the entire universe could be understood. Before the Principia, science had been a haphazard enterprise of scattered observations. After it, men and women could dream of understanding everything—that one day scientific knowledge could be so complete that there would be nothing that couldn't be predicted.

The Royal Society was awed. Hooke responded with characteristic jealousy, accusing Newton of plagiarism. Halley responded with characteristic generosity; when it turned out that the Society had wasted its printing budget for the year on a catalog of fish species, Halley funded the Principia's first printing out of his own pocket. But the reactions of Hooke, Halley, and every other fellow had one thing in common: they all understood that Newton had just changed their world forever.

How such an extraordinary mind came to be—and the many gifts it left for us all—is the story of this book.

Introduction

"I do not know what I may appear to the world, but to myself I seem to have been only like a boy playing on the seashore, and diverting myself in now and then finding a smoother pebble or a prettier shell than ordinary, whilst the great ocean of truth lay all undiscovered before me."

- Isaac Newton

While the above quote portrays the child-like innocence of the great man and speaks volumes of his humility, in reality, Newton had a less fortunate childhood. Born in a remote village without the nurturing care of a loving parent, he never held back from speaking his mind. He argued bitterly when instigated, worked in secrecy, and even turned towards self-imposed isolation for long periods. Despite this, he discovered and achieved more than anyone could have conceived, both before and after his time.

Newton was a pioneer, and laid roads that generations have followed in the centuries after his death. Everything that he explored and explained serves as the quintessential model for theoretical and applied science today. His legacy stands as the groundwork and bedrock for a variety of scientific disciplines, and without his influence, the work of dozens of notable scientists and inventors from Tesla to Einstein may have never been completed.

Despite the monolithic quality of his work, Newton appeared to have regarded his discoveries as merely the solutions to unresolved puzzles. He deciphered complex concepts of light and motion, discovered gravity, explained the course of heavenly bodies, and helped humanity recognize and grasp its place in the cosmos. He encouraged debate and challenged uncertainty. He was, is, and will always be considered the chief architect of the modern world.

Chapter 1:
The Birth of a Genius

"Genius is patience."

- Isaac Newton

Birth and Early Childhood

In 1623, amidst a chaotic civil war, early modern England was far from the peaceful place it is today. Nestled on a hill near the Witham River laid a hallmark ranch, also known as the Woolsthorpe farmhouse. With its short front door, secured windows, functional kitchen and bare floors, the farmhouse was one of the few houses that was made out of limestone— a symbol of luxury when compared to the more common clay and hay huts. Today, that house is known for one other reason - it is the birthplace of the most influential scientist in history.

It is in this year that Robert Newton, a yeoman farmer and the grandfather of Isaac Newton, bought the manor. His son, who was also called

Isaac, followed in the family tradition, and became a relatively prosperous yeoman farmer. By 1642, the Woolsthorpe manor had belonged to the Newton ancestors for nearly twenty years. In the backyard stood the famous apple tree that Newton later described as the place he discovered the concept of gravity.

According to the Julian Calendar, Newton was born on December 25, 1642, to his namesake and his mother, Hannah Ayscough. Newton was born prematurely, and under rather unhappy conditions. Three months before his birth, Isaac senior had passed away, and Hannah was faced with raising her son on her own.

Hannah chose to abandon young Isaac to his maternal grandmother when he was three. She remarried a wealthy man named Barnabas Smith in return for a small piece of land in her son's name. Without the love and guidance from stable parents, Newton spent his childhood angry most of the time, and even threatened to his mother and step-father's house while they were inside.

Abandoned by his mother and left under the care of his maternal grandmother, Newton had a lonely childhood. The fact that he had lost his father before birth, was abandoned by his mother at the age of three, had no siblings to play with, and was not close to his grandmother made the young man rebellious in many ways. As the years passed by, he also became more and more aloof and reserved. By the time he was ten, his mother had given birth to three more children with her second husband, and had unfortunately been widowed a second time. It was only then that Hannah decided to move back into the Woolsthorpe farmhouse with her three other children. Newton later insisted that he was happy that he had his mother back, despite their tumultuous relationship.

As a result of this reunion, Newton acquired his stepfather's library of nearly three hundred theological books. He later stated that reading those very books provided him with some of the answers that he had sought, and cited them as what had given him both the thirst for knowledge and love for reading.

Early School Days

Newton was exceptionally bright and stood out from the crowd, even as a child. When he was still a student at the King's School, he was greatly influenced by the lessons taught by Henry Stokes, a schoolmaster who taught students Latin, Theology, Greek, and Hebrew. Much of the curriculum was geared towards agricultural pursuits. Stokes, in the hope that his lessons would empower his students to be highly efficient and self-sufficient farmers, Stokes included practical arithmetic, and taught his students ways to measure the areas of shapes. He taught them algorithms for surveying, marking, and calculating acreage. He also taught them how to inscribe regular polygons in a circle and compute the length of each side. Not only did young Newton grasp these concepts quickly, he excelled at them.

The First Flashes of Genius

Newton later recounted the way sunlight crept along the walls of his house on most bright days. He noticed that the sun's rays cast slanted edges against the walls as they passed through the window. These slant edges shifted between sharp and bright images, and revealed a three-dimensional view of intersecting planes.

Intrigued by it, the young man constructed crude figures of circles and arches in an attempt to measure time. He measured small distances with strings and compounded calculations that converted inches to minutes in an hour. As years passed by and he learned more about mathematics and the solar system, he grew consciously aware of the pattern in which the sun rose and fell each day. He also noticed how its position shifted slightly against the stars every year. Newton later realized that these changes were the result of the earth's elliptical orbit around the sun.

The Second and Third and...

During his school years, Newton was intrigued by the construction of a windmill at the top of Gonerby Hill, situated on the Great North Road. During this time, windmills were fairly uncommon, as most areas used watermills. Fascinated by the sight, Newton observed and tracked its progress for several days. Determined to learn more about it, he built a replica of it. He used cloth for the sails and fixed it to the roof of the house. Understanding the need for adequate wind in order for his replica to turn, he constructed a wheel that, when turned, generated wind. His pet mouse— which he named Mouse Miller— was used to turn the wheel.

Further demonstrating his adolescent inventiveness, Newton also made a small lantern out of paper in order to light his way along the path to school during dark winter mornings. He was able to fold it up and keep it in his pocket during school hours, and on at least one instance he strung it to a kite to scare his neighbors.

Back to Woolsthorpe Manor

In 1659, when Newton was 17, his mother summoned him back home. The war had ended, and Hannah wanted her son to learn more about the farm. Although Newton had excelled at school, she wanted him to carry on the family business and become a farmer. Despite Newton's lack of interest, she pulled him out of formal schooling and initiated him into farming practices.

Although he went through the ordeal for a short while, Newton later recalled that he disliked farming. He recounted that once, while he was asked to watch sheep, he built model water mills with dams in a stream. The sheep he was supposed to watch over, which remained free and unwatched, strayed into a neighbor's corn field and damaged it, leaving his mother with no choice but to pay for the damages.

In his famous list of sins, he wrote that the nine months he spent trying to learn farming were particularly unhappy for him, and that his discontent with his situation caused him to disobey his mother and quarrel with his step-sister. Perhaps sensing his dislike for farming and his inherent intellectual abilities, Isaac's uncle, a graduate from Cambridge University, persuaded his sister to send her son back to school. Hannah eventually capitulated, recognizing her son's unhappiness, and sent him on to school.

Chapter 2:
Entry into the World of Science

"To me there has never been a higher source of earthly honor or distinction than that connected with advances in science."

- Isaac Newton

Early Influences and Later Years

Although Newton was sent to school, his mother offered no financial support. To make ends meet, Newton had to make his way through college by performing demanding chores. While most students his age led a socially active life, Newton rarely socialized and instead pursued his thirst for knowledge. In the course of this pursuit, he came across the philosophies of modern French philosopher René Descartes, whose ideologies on the wave theory of light he later challenged.

Descartes propagated a mechanical philosophy of science, and believed that the mind and body are distinct entities that coexist— a thesis that was later termed "mind-body dualism." Newton was influenced by the French philosopher's view, and began to look at the individual elements that made up the world. He regarded the world as an amalgamation of various bodies coexisting in harmony, and studied the nature of these individual bodies— the precursor to quantum physics.

As the years passed by, Newton's interest in modern science grew, particularly in quantum and particle science. This pursuit brought him into contact with Isaac Barrow— a fellow Cambridge professor whose role Newton eventually succeeded.

Time at Cambridge

On June 5th 1661, upon the recommendation of his uncle, Isaac Newton was admitted to Trinity

College in Cambridge. Although he started as a subsizar (someone who partially paid for his education), within a matter of three years, he was awarded a scholarship that guaranteed him four more years of study.

Newton's time at Cambridge was in the middle of the literary and scientific revolution of the 17th century. Astronomers such as Copernicus and Kepler had conceived the heliocentric view of the universe. The theory that was so insightful and revolutionary that it paved the way for further study, and was later refined by Galileo.

During this time, the scientific world was abuzz with new concepts, and the authors of these theories gained immense popularity amid European theoretical circles. Theorist Rene Descartes had disclosed his idea of nature as a complex, neutral, and exclusive entity, for example. Despite growing support, Cambridge continued to preach the traditional and qualitative views of Aristotelian philosophies, as most universities of the time did. They believed that nature rested on a geocentric view of the universe.

While Newton was taught the standard curriculum of conventional physics, he spent most of his free time reading books that were authored by modern philosophers. In fact, it was during this time that Newton kept a journal titled Quaestiones Quaedam Philosophicae, roughly translating to "Certain Philosophical Questions." Later, a close look at the journal revealed that Newton might have discovered concepts of nature that eventually provided the framework for the scientific revolution.

In 1664, Cambridge hired a professor of mathematics for the first time in its history. Isaac Barrow, a former Trinity College student himself and a little over nine years older than

Newton, became the first occupant of the Lucasian chair at Cambridge. Barrow had studied Greek and theology before moving onto medicine, church history, and geometry.

Soon enough, Newton attended Barrow's lectures and was drawn to his lessons. Later that year, Barrow examined Newton's view over the elements of Euclid, concepts that were relatively new to Newton. However, Newton was no stranger to learning and mastering new concepts. He bought and borrowed books, and pursued knowledge outside the standard curriculum whenever possible. Soon enough, Newton invented new concepts in his mind just as he absorbed and mastered older ones. He faired exceptionally well in his thesis, and earned the respect of Barrow for life.

Although Newton successfully completed his bachelor's degree in 1665, he was forced to return home in August of that year while the

University closed down in precaution against a great plague. Undaunted, he continued to study at home, and in the next few years he developed his theories on calculus, optics, and the law of gravitation. In fact, it was in the Woolsthorpe farmhouse that the idea of universal gravitation first occurred to him, as he watched an apple drop to the ground in his garden.

In 1667, once the epidemic was over, Newton returned to Cambridge as a fellow of Trinity and acquired his master's degree in 1668. During this time, he came across a book published by Nicholas Mercator. The book addressed and provoked new concepts that dealt with the infinite series, an important mathematical concept. Intrigued by it, Newton wrote a paper that spoke about his wider views on the topic. However, instead of owning authorship, he chose not to publish the book.

Instead, he shared it with his friend and mentor, Isaac Barrow.

In 1670 at the age of twenty-seven, Newton became the professor of Mathematics at Trinity College. The following three years saw Newton age rapidly; his uncombed and shoulder-length hair became grey, he lost weight until he was exceptionally thin, and his shoulders drooped. At thirty, he looked much older than his age, and behaved much wiser too.

During his professional years, Newton continued to teach, inspire, and explain the concepts that he'd mastered. He also remained strikingly private, and welcomed friendship with only a selected few. He was careless of meals, and often worked late into the evening by candlelight. He stayed isolated in his chamber for long hours, even days sometimes. The few times that he chose to dine in the hall, he was left undisturbed at the table— by many accounts, Newton often scowled when he was bothered during meals, and his fellows thought it best to avoid confronting his preoccupied mind.

While a professor at Cambridge University, Newton was excused from tutoring or conducting classes, but was required to deliver annual lectures. During one such lecture, he chose to speak about the properties of light. He claimed that it was made up of particles and not waves, challenging the prevailing belief of the time.

Adherents to the wave theory of light believed that light is made up of waves comprised of white light. They also argued that the color spectrum (which is visible when a beam of light passes through a prism) is caused due to a corruption in the glass. Newton, on the other hand, argued that light is made up of particles, and that the color spectrum is caused by light itself. Robert Hooke, a fellow philosopher and architect, believed in the wave theory of light and strongly debated against Newton's theory. This debate remained unresolved for over a century.

"Have not the small Particles of Bodies certain Powers, Virtues or Forces, by which they act at a distance, not only upon the Rays of Light for reflecting, refracting and reflecting them, but also upon one another for producing a great part of the Phænomena of Nature?"

1669 - The Year of Invention and Isolation

In 1669, Newton received a letter of general correspondence from the Royal Society. The letter was an invitation for members to contribute. Over a series of correspondence,

Robert Hooke, the man who challenged Newton's particle theory of light, brought up a question on planetary motion. Hooke believed that a formula involving inverse squares might help explain the attraction between planets and the shape of their orbits. Newton responded with his answer, but broke off the correspondence before they came to a substantial conclusion. Secluded and alone once again, Newton applied Hooke's theory and found compelling answers to the problem. In fact, he even resolved the ambiguity that surrounded the topic. Newton kept the records hidden from everyone, including the person whose theory he had partially used. No account of why he chose to conceal such a revolutionary concept of astrophysics exists.

The death of his mother during this year caused an emotional void in Newton, and he chose to withdraw from public speeches for six long years. He became particularly isolated and kept conversations and interactions to a bare minimum. During this time, he pursued his study of gravity, and eventually understood the effects it had on orbits and planets.

It was in the same year that Newton invented his very own telescope. However, he also chose to keep this invention hidden from the world for two years, and only revealed it to Barrow in 1671.

In 1669, Barrow shared the unaccredited document (Newton's views on the infinite series) authored by Newton with British mathematician John Collins. Later in August 1669, Barrow disclosed the book's author to Collins as "Mr. Newton— a fellow of our College, and very young... but of an extraordinary genius and proficient in these things."

Despite Being a Professor, His Hiatus from Public Life Continued

Word spread through Collins. Newton's work quickly gained attention and appreciation among mathematicians. Shortly afterward, the mentor made way for his prodigious student, and Barrow resigned his post as professor so that Newton could succeed him. From this point on, Newton became a prominent face in the scientific world. He became Lucasian Professor of Mathematics in 1669, and successfully held the position for three years. Despite this recognition, he remained withdrawn and reserved for most periods.

Several years later, while the debate on the particle and wave theory of light continued, Newton used his newly-discovered concepts of refraction and diffraction to strengthen his case. However, as his concepts went against the traditional views of Aristotle, they were not received well by the Royal Society of Science. In fact, the topic sparked a long debate that remained inconclusive for over a century, long past Newton's time.

A Life Amid Isolation and Secrecy

Newton spent the next ten years researching and devising his laws of motion and gravity. He also used this hiatus to master concepts of calculus and the infinite series. In 1684, in a conversation with fellow Trinity members Christopher Wren and Edmond Halley, Hooke reiterated his theory on planetary motion. However, with no mathematical proof and no correspondence from Newton, Hooke had little to prove his case. In August of that year, a few months after Hooke's second attempt, Edmond

Halley visited Newton at Cambridge and asked him about his views on the shape of planetary orbits with regards to Hooke's theory. Newton finally revealed to Halley that, several years prior to this, he had proven that planetary orbits were elliptical.

In 1687, with the help of Halley— who bore all expenses of publishing and correcting the manuscript— Newton published his incredibly popular book, titled The Philosophic Naturalis Principia Mathematica. It was in this book that he explained universal gravitation and the three laws of motion— all of which dominated the scientific view of the physical universe for the next three centuries.

In 1692, a few years after he published Principia, Newton suffered the loss of certain personal and scientific journals, that nature of which are still unknown. What is clear is that due to the loss of his journals, which were likely records of his research over the previous two decades, he suffered a nervous breakdown that lasted for nearly two long years.

Thankfully, when he emerged from this isolation, he was received with accolades and respect for his other scholarly works. In 1699, Newton was accepted as a member of the French Académie des Sciences, and in 1703 he was elected President of the Royal Society of Science.

A Book on Light

In 1704, at the age of 61, Newton authored and published the book Optiks, in which he explained and elaborated on his particle theory of light. In the book, he analyzed the essential nature of light and explored concepts of refraction and diffraction in explicit detail. Newton explained the refraction of light as it passes through mediums such as prisms and lenses. He also explained the diffraction of light when it passes through tightly-spaced sheets of glass. Finally, he explained the behavior of color combinations by using spectral lights or pigment powders to deduce the mixtures. In his book, Newton also questioned the claims of Aristotle, who believed that pure light (such as the light from the sun) is fundamentally white or colorless, and is transformed into color when in contact with darkness or matter. Newton believed that the reverse of this concept is true— that light is composed of different spectral shades which are differentiated into seven colors— red, orange, yellow, green, blue, indigo, and violet— and that all colors, including white, are formed by numerous combinations of these shades.

The next year, the Royal Society appointed him as the Warden of the Mint, and he later became the Master of the Royal Mint. With a new purpose, Newton soon retired from his professorship at Cambridge and pursued his work at the Mint. He spent his remaining years working there, and made significant contributions to currency reforms. In the early 1700's, when the country was going through a shortage of currency circulation, Newton proposed and oversaw radical changes in his role as Master of the Mint. He reprinted smaller denominations of currency and enforced laws to ensure financial stability. In 1705, he earned a knighthood from Queen Anne for his incredible contributions.

In 1708, back at Woolsthorpe, the stars, moon, and the apple tree rooted at his backyard continued to inspire and occupy the mind of sixty-five year old Newton. Theology, mathematics, physics, and Alchemy were all inhabitants of his beautiful mind. He continued to document everything that his complex mind explored and conquered. He wrote in silence and isolation without ever feeling the need to tell anyone; rather, he studied merely for its own sake rather than for self-aggrandizement.

Despite further signs of emotional breakdown, in 1714, the genius (now in his early seventies) had clear eyesight and memory. He continued to read, calculate, and debate the things that occupied his mind. He also remained gentle and modest, although aloof and isolated.

"A man may imagine things that are false, but he can only understand things that are true, for if the things be false, the apprehension of them is not understanding."

Newton's Death

In March of 1727, after hours of agonizing pain, the great man died from a stone in his bladder. He neither cried out nor complained, but seemed to embrace death. Newton's passing resulted in a decade-long outcry of condolences and poetic verses from both the literary world and common people. Newton had earned a permanent place in everyone's heart, landed gentry and working class alike. A few centuries after his death, the great man's legacy still inspires the lives of many, just as he did when he was alive. He was, after all, the philosopher of light.

Chapter 3:
A Glimpse into a
Beautiful Mind

"My powers are ordinary. Only my application brings me success."

- Isaac Newton

Isaac the Individual

According to historical records, Newton always appeared to be a loner of sorts, and was known to be extremely protective of his privacy. Even while he was at the peak of his career and had achieved well-deserved recognition and honors, Newton remained an extremely guarded and temperamental person, and allegedly was known for bouts of outbursts and violent temper when provoked.

He believed learning was a worthy pursuit in its own regard. He cared for little else but knowledge. He wrote voraciously, but only shared his work with others when he was certain that it was the truth; he did not take his knowledge for granted. He challenged every article he wrote and every idea he conceived until he was certain he'd arrived at the ultimate truth. Simply put, he wrote to reason, to reflect, to communicate, and just to humor his expansive mind.

His father was a reasonably successful farmer. The older Newton worked the land of Woolsthorpe, and built a substantial dwelling made out of limestone— considered to be a sign of luxury. His son instead pursued science, and achieved much, much more. The fact that he received a full state funeral, an honor usually reserved for monarchs, remains a testimony to the profound achievement and following the great scientist had accomplished in his lifetime.

With no particular mentors to look up to other than his friend Barrow, he pursued his thirst for knowledge and moved from topic to topic on his own. He broke down complex theories into simple and comprehensible laws that could be applied for definite results. He taught that knowledge was not something to be blindly followed, but a thing to be deliberated until its results were quantitative and exact enough to be considered the truth. He was an institution by himself, and left behind a wealth of knowledge that continues to intrigue, challenge, and motivate intellectuals.

In essence, Newton revolutionized science like never before. He taught that it was okay to question and challenge all that was uncertain and all that was blindly followed as the norm. His laws of motion and gravitation form the basis of space travel. He explained complex concepts in the field of mathematics, and was one of two possible founders of calculus. Isaac Newton was a man of few words and of impeccable intellect. Simply put, he was a visionary, the first of his kind, and second to none.

Lack of Personal Accounts

Although the intellectual works of Newton continue to influence and dominate the modern world, very little is known of his private life. Newton maintained no personal journals, only scientific ones, and spent most of his time compounding complex mathematical calculations or observing the qualities of light in solitude. Much of his works did not receive their due, or otherwise remained unpublished during his lifetime. While he explored mathematics and conceived the calculus (a mathematical study of change), while he poured through the most secret of sciences, alchemy, and designed principles that are now referred to as the laws of motion and gravity, he did so mostly in isolation and kept much of it hidden from the outside world. To most people he remained a stranger till his end, long after he'd gained recognition and was honored with the title "Sir."

While there are plenty of secondary and tertiary accounts that discuss Newton's personality and early years, there are only a handful of journals that are written from his own pen. The most valuable of them is his book of sins, published in 1662. In the book, as a student at the Trinity College in Cambridge, a 19-year old Newton catalogued the sins he had committed in his lifetime. Written in confidentiality, the book provides a captivating glimpse into his mind. What stands out is the simplicity and childlike innocence of the great man. While he might have revolutionized the modern world with his theories, at heart, beneath the quiet and guarded personality, was a man whose demons were harmless and short.

His sins are listed below:

Before Whitsunday 1662:

1. Using the word (God) openly

2. Eating an apple at Thy house

3. Making a feather while on Thy day

4. Denying that I made it.

5. Making a mousetrap on Thy day

6. Contriving of the chimes on Thy day

7. Squirting water on Thy day

8. Making pies on Sunday night

9. Swimming in a kimnel on Thy day

10. Putting a pin in Iohn Keys hat on Thy day to pick him

11. Carelessly hearing and committing many sermons

12. Refusing to go to the close at my mother's command

13. Threatening my father and mother Smith to burn them and the house over them

14. Wishing death and hoping it to some

15. Striking many

16. Having unclean thoughts, words, actions and dreams

17. Stealing cherry cobs from Eduard Storer

18. Denying that I did so

19. Denying a crossbow to my mother and grandmother though I knew of it

20. Setting my heart on money learning pleasure more than Thee

21. A relapse

22. A relapse

23. A breaking again of my covenant renued in the Lords Supper

24. Punching my sister

25. Robbing my mothers box of plums and sugar

26. Calling Dorothy Rose a jade

27. Gluttony in my sickness

28. Peevishness with my mother

29. With my sister

30. Falling out with the servants

31. Divers commissions of alle my duties

32. Idle discourse on Thy day and at other times

33. Not turning nearer to Thee for my affections

34. Not living according to my belief

35. Not loving Thee for Thy self

36.   Not loving Thee for Thy goodness to us

37. Not desiring Thy ordinances

38. Not long {longing} for Thee in {illeg}

39.   Fearing man above Thee

40.   Using unlawful means to bring us out of distresses

41. Caring for worldly things more than God

42. Not craving a blessing from God on our honest endeavours.

43. Missing chapel.

44. Beating Arthur Storer.

45. Peevishness at Master Clarks for a piece of bread and butter.

46. Striving to cheat with a brass halfe crowne.

47. Twisting a cord on Sunday morning

48. Reading the history of the Christian champions on Sunday

Since Whitsunday 1662:

1. Gluttony
2. Gluttony
3. Using Wilfords towel to spare my own
4. Negligence at the chapel
5. Sermons at Saint Marys (4)
6. Lying about a louse
7. Denying my chamberfellow of the knowledge of him that took him for a sot.
8. Neglecting to pray 3
9. Helping Pettit to make his water watch at 12 of the clock on Saturday night.

Newton's Views on Aristotle, Plato and God

His quote "If I have seen further than others, it is by standing upon the shoulders of giants" and "Plato is my friend; Aristotle is my friend, but my greatest friend is truth," implies that he competed with no one but himself, though he gave credit where it was due. He never intended to break rules, nor did he ignore the occult knowledge that was prevalent in his time. He never disputed the existence of God, and even went on to say that "In the absence of any other proof, the thumb alone would convince me of God's existence." His only quest was for knowledge and a sense of completion when he considered anything that appeared uncertain and doubtful to him.

Chapter 4:
Conflicting Thoughts on Light

"Colors which appear from the prism are to be derived from the light of the white one."

- Isaac Newton

A Vital Experiment

In 1667, roughly a year after Italian physicist Grimaldi published his work on diffraction, Newton claimed that he could challenge Descartes's wave theory of light with the help of his first prism. Newton believed that Descartes's theory was merely a possibility of refraction, which is the way that waves— in this case, light— bend when they pass from a faster medium to a slower one. He further argued that waves do not travel in straight lines, and that in order to explain the geometric nature of the laws of reflection and refraction, light must first be perceived as comprised of particles. He termed these particles "corpuscles."

A Debate Begins

Newton's claim gave birth to a revolutionary concept, but also stirred up a lengthy debate that lasted for several years among those who supported the wave theory. A few years later, after joining the Royal Society of London in 1672, Newton stated that the 44th attempt in a series of experiments he had conducted earlier that year had proven that which he had claimed before— that light is made of particles, and not waves.

Followers of Descartes's wave theory claimed that light waves are comprised of white light alone, and that the color spectrum, which can be seen when light passes through a prism, is formed due to a corruption in the glass medium. They further stated that the more glass mediums the light travels through, the more corrupted the glass becomes and the more colors one is likely to see.

However, when Newton, in an attempt to prove that the theory was wrong, passed a beam of pure white light through two identical prisms, both of which were held at exact angles, the light split into a spectrum of colors when passing through the first prism, and then recomposed itself back into white light as it traversed through the second. This experiment clearly indicated that the light spectrum seen was not a consequence of corrupted glass.

Newton believed that his newfound discovery was a crucial experiment. He considered it an experiment that was potent enough to debate and challenge Descartes's contradictory wave theory of light. As most scientists of the time believed that light was either made up of particles or waves, Newton used the failure of the wave theory to prove that light must be made up of particles. Hoping to prove his point and rest the case, he further claimed that light is composed of minute colored particles that, when merged, appear white.

Dissecting the Color Spectrum

Having stated that light is made up of particles and not waves, Newton demonstrated the properties of light with regards to the color spectrum. Although the spectrum of light appears continuous and with no distinct boundaries between adjacent colors, Newton chose to catalogue light into seven colors and introduce them as "the color spectrum." Some scientists believe that Newton recognized the mystical property of the number 7, mostly due to its relationship between the seven wandering stars and the seven days in a week, and hence chose the mystical number for his significant theory. Newton classified the colors as red, orange, yellow, green, blue, indigo, and violet—also recognized as the colors seen in a rainbow.

He proved that every color had a unique angle of refraction that could be calculated with a suitable prism. He deduced that the color of objects was a result of light refraction. He also believed that a beam of colored light retains its properties of color irrespective of the number of times it is reflected or refracted. With this, he proved that color is a property of light reflected from objects as opposed to the idea that it was the property of the object itself. This ran counter to the wave theory, which postulated that objects held the necessary properties to form colored light.

When All Did Not Go Well With the Royal Society

Despite his confidence in his theory, it faced stark criticism and was not readily accepted. Within a year, a debate broke out when fellow Royal Society member Robert Hooke published results that supported Grimaldi's theory of diffraction. He debated that, contrary to what Newton claimed, diffraction was not a type of refraction, and that it could only be explained when light was seen as a wave. Hooke explained that when light travels in a vacuum or other uniform mediums, they form wave-like peaks that move in an upward-downward direction. He believed the peaks form surfaces that resembled the layers of an onion. Hooke further claimed that they were spherical and spread out to form waves as they travelled at the speed of light. He believed his theory explained that light passing through an opening spread out as waves rather than particle-like substances, as Newton had claimed.

What followed was a conflict of theories. While some members supported Hooke and criticized Newton's particle theory, some disputed the existence of the color spectrum. There were others who rejected his claim that the 44th attempt proved that light is not comprised of waves. Additionally, those who tried to replicate the experiment in their attempt to support Newton failed to do so.

Back then, prisms were merely viewed as objects of entertainment, and were not commonly accepted as scientific instruments. Venetian glass, commonly regarded as the standard against which other glasses were compared, had its share of defects and flaws. Unfortunately, Newton did little to resolve the confusion, and concealed the details of his experiment. While he displayed the authenticity of his experiment by displaying the spectrum of colors through a prism, he did not explain the process of generating a spectrum from the first prism, or the exact dimensions of the second.

In fact, it was not until 1676— four years after the first presentation— that Newton revealed substantial information for people to replicate it. It was only then that he revealed that the clearest and most appropriate prisms to use were the ones manufactured in London, and not the ones commonly imported from Italy. However, this information provided little or no help in replicating the experiment. Scientists continued to fail the experiment irrespective of the type of prism they used, and this eventually tempted Newton to withdraw from the debate.

The Debate Continues

In 1678, barely a year after the last debate, Dutch mathematician Christiaan Huygens claimed that he had disproven Newton's theory by proving that the laws of reflection and refraction can be drawn from the wave theory of light. Huygens claimed that diffraction occurs as a result of the interference caused between wave fronts. He stated that when light is projected through a small opening, waves are pushed together at various angles, creating fringes and noisy patterns of light and dark shadows.

To elaborate on this point, he compared the contrasting properties of light and water waves when passed through a small gap. Huygens believed that light waves and water waves are similar but for one aspect alone: the direction in which they move. He believed that water waves were two-directional, and stated that water waves move up and down like a sine wave while water moved forward. Light waves, on the contrary, were believed to move in one direction alone: forward and in the direction of the beam.

Then, in an attempt to draw similarities, he compared light waves to sound waves. Sound waves, similar to light waves, are longitudinal waves, and hence move forward and in one direction only. He claimed that while sound waves moved forward, they periodically displace tiny parts of molecules in the air. He argued that while this was so, the molecules constituting the sound waves merely vibrate, and do not move forward.

Therefore, for light to move through space as a wave, it must have a medium through which to pass. This meant that Huygens's theory, like all theories of light before it, was dependent upon Aristotle's concept of aether, the fifth element (that which represents the upper sky, mainly space and heaven). Despite this, there remained one concept that Huygens's theory of light could not explain: Bartholin's calcite crystals.

Back in 1669, roughly three years before Newton first challenged the wave theory with his particle theory of light, physicist Erasmus Bartholin chanced upon some calcite crystals in Iceland and began experimenting with them. During his experimentation, he discovered that images placed behind the crystal were duplicated, with one copy slightly above the other. When he rotated the crystal, Bartholin noticed that while one image disappeared, the other rotated with the crystal. This made him believe that the crystal had properties that split the beam of light into two different rays. He referred to it as "one of the greatest wonders that nature has produced."

This concept disputed Huygens's wave theory of light in the future. In an attempt to explain this contradictory theory, Huygens claimed that the crystals could have been made up of two distinct materials— one that produced spherical waves, and another that produced ellipsoidal ones, both of which were viewed from a two-dimensional perspective. However, when he placed images behind crystals that were placed adjacent to each other, the number of images duplicated varied with respect to the position of the crystals, both independently and interdependently. This dynamic property of light waves when subjected to crystal mediums went against his concept of wave theory, and Huygens ultimately failed to explain it.

Newton Uses the Failed Explanation to Strengthen His Debate

When Huygens was unable to explain the relationship between Bartholin's calcite crystals and the wave theory, Newton was quick to prove that the calcite experiment showed that light has sides— something that could be easily explained by his corpuscular theory. Newton also referred to his book Optiks, which analyzed the fundamental properties of light with respect to refraction and diffraction, to defend and strengthen his views on diffraction. However, while doing so, he stated that particles of light create waves in aether, meaning that although light waves displayed wave-like qualities, they were made up of tiny particles only. While this theory, along with his book, gained immense popularity among the scientific fraternity, it continued to be a bone of contention amongst those who remained unconvinced.

The Final Verdict

Newton, along with other intellectuals of the time, believed there was only one way to derive the answer. If light was made up of particles as Newton believed, then it should travel faster when passed through a thicker medium. However, if it is composed of waves as Descartes and Huygens believed, then the speed at which it moved while travelling through denser mediums should be relatively slow.

While this might have put things into perspective and settled a long-fought debate, the experiment was not conducted for another 150 years, and remained inconclusive during Newton's lifetime.

Interestingly, it turned out that both Newton and his critics were correct; light is both particle and wave, and its dual nature served to frustrate scientists for centuries.

Chapter 5:

Newton's Reflector

"My Design in this book is not to explain the Properties of Light by Hypotheses, but to propose and prove them by Reason and Experiments."

- Isaac Newton

The Invention of the Telescope

In the 17th century, the scientific world buzzed with discoveries that could help them understand the universe a little more closely. The invention of the telescope by Hans Lippershey in 1608 gave scientists a whole new perspective.

The invention spurred intense interest in people. Everyone who could lay their hands on the device was eager to know what the universe above looked like from close quarters. It also inspired people to think about light and color like never before. However, the telescope had one flaw: its field of view was particularly small. Astronomers were keen to use the telescope to study planets and the solar system. However, given that it had a narrow field of view, the telescope could not be used to view distant objects adequately. They needed something that could help them see the universe under restricted light and in clear view.

In order to see distant objects such as stars and planets in faint light, telescopes capture additional light to compensate for the lack of natural light. Astronomers needed a bigger lens that could capture far more light than the smaller ones used in the telescopes of their time. The purpose of this lens is to focus light onto a single point or object. When it is channeled in one direction and on one object alone, the image seen through the viewfinder will be clear and in focus.

The improved telescope had a wider field of view, but the images produced were blurry and out of focus. This new problem was a persistent conundrum for scientists, who could not determine the cause of the blur.

Meanwhile in 1669, amidst the silence that filled his lonely and isolated room, the 26 year old Newton was busy in the company of that which currently occupied his brilliant mind. Grieving the death of his mother, Isaac had turned towards books and ideas for solace. He poured through books on gravity, and held a keen interest in astronomy. He was particularly interested in ways to explain the orbital motions of planets. He also drew a keen interest in the field of physics. Having already acquired in-depth knowledge in the field of mathematics, he used his mathematical knowledge to deduce answers to problems in physics.

He studied the telescope and reflected on the reasons for its blurred out images. He doggedly pursued the issue until he understood the root cause for the problem. Soon enough, Newton discovered something that he believed would change the perception of optical science in the future. Newton discovered that shining light through a piece of glass bends the light and splits it into different colors. A similar process takes place when light is passed through a glass lens. The lens brings each color into focus, but at a different length or point. Therefore, as light splits into the seven different colors, they converge at multiple points and cause the image to blur. The bigger the lens, the more points of light it can focus, and the more distorted the image is likely to appear.

This experiment led him to understand a fundamental property of light itself. Newton considered the phenomenon of refraction and believed he had found the answers to the problems with the telescope. He had devised a solution that, when applied, would allow telescope views to be perfectly clear. However, in order to demonstrate and explain the solution, Newton needed a device that could reflect light in its true form. Since Lippershey's telescope distorted images, it could not be used for his experiment. Therefore, Newton had only one option left in front of him— he decided to create his very own telescope.

In 1668, he first constructed a prototype of what he later called the "reflector," also known as "Newton's reflector." Newton calculated and drew measurements to allow this reflector to fit his telescope design, and ground and polished the concave lenses himself.

Through his research, Newton understood light like no one else had. He realized that the problem was not in the imperfect crafting of the lenses, but was a result of the very nature of white light. He saw light as something much more than the pure white form that most people believed it to be. To him, light was not simple but complex, not pure but varied; light was a heterogeneous mixture of differently colored rays.

Determined to prove that his theory was right, he made changes to his old telescope and built a new one. He built the device out of a mirror, a wooden ball, and some wooden tubes. To start with, he removed the large and troublesome lens, and replaced it with something entirely different— a metal disk shaped into a concave mirror that he polished until it was as smooth as glass. Using his furnace, he refined its surface. By the end of 1669, he had assembled a telescope that magnified objects forty times more than the best telescopes in London and Italy.

The use of a mirror instead of the conventional lens revolutionized the mechanics of the device permanently. The mirror reflected distant objects to a single point. A second, smaller mirror connected to the view finder bounced the light into the eyepiece. With all of that light focused into the eyepiece, not only was there enough light to view the image clearly, but there was also no separation of colors to distort or blur the image. By reflecting the light from objects, Newton's telescope captured sharp images of even the most distant objects. The results were clear and factual.

However, Newton chose not to share the news of his invention with the rest of the world. Instead, he kept it to himself for two years. Through it, he viewed the rings of Jupiter with its satellites. He viewed the four Galilean moons. He observed the crescent face of Venus, and also noticed that it was similar to the size of Earth. By 1671, Newton had constructed a second reflector that was even better, constructing a device that was far, far ahead of its time.

Although he enjoyed the spectacular views of the planets and beyond through his telescope, Newton did so in secrecy. It was only in late 1671 (long after he had constructed his second telescope) that Newton shared his invention with his mentor Barrow.

As expected, the device revolutionized the study of planetary objects and took the world by storm. Newton's small and simple reflector was far more powerful and accurate than the conventional telescope, which towered at six feet. Marveled by its significance and accuracy, Barrow revealed it to the world and to the Royal Society of Science in particular. However, like several of Newton's other inventions and discoveries, this was not well-received at first. Although the Royal Society recognized the incredible potential of the device, they were strictly averse to the fact that it was hidden in secrecy for years.

Like every institution before it, the Royal Society was born with its virtues rooted deeply in conventional beliefs. The institution encouraged communication and condemned secrecy. Fellow members pledged to share their ideas with the collective society. They believed that science does not exist as an organization or as an activity, but existed as an outcome of the thoughts conceived by society and the public. They believed in the principles of their founding fathers. "So far are the narrow conceptions of a few private Writers, in a dark Age, from being equal to so vast a design," their founders declared.

"I keep the subject of my inquiry constantly before me, and wait till the first dawning opens gradually, by little and little, into a full and clear light."

Mixed Emotions

Just as always, Newton's latest invention received mixed support. There were people who were greatly impacted by it and therefore argued in its favor. There were others who felt shunned by the secrecy with which the device was invented, and hence opposed it. While some skilled examiners agreed that Newton's telescope magnified images more than any other conventional telescope present at that time, others chose to be indifferent, and claimed there was no way to measure its accuracy with utmost certainty. However, irrespective of whether people poured in support or scorned it in disdain, one thing was certain: from this point on, telescopes evolved by virtue of their mirrors, and not their lenses.

Meanwhile, far away in Cambridge, Newton endured the impact of his latest invention, but remained unaffected by it. In late 1671, a few months after the telescope had been made public to the world, Newton received a letter from Henry Oldenburg, a German and fellow member of the Royal Society.

In it, Oldenburg sought Newton's permission to publish an account of the reflecting telescope, but promised to attribute all credits to Newton himself. "It being too frequent, the new Inventions and contrivances are snatched away from their true Authors by pretending bystanders," he wrote. Oldenburg also offered membership to the Royal Society for his latest invention. He urged Newton to accept the invitation as he feared other foreigners might plagiarize the device or take claim of the revolutionary invention.

Many scientists all over the world sought a chance to engrave their names in the history books for eternity. Robert Hooke, the man who repeatedly opposed Newton's corpuscular theory, was no different, and wanted to claim his share of the limelight too. He told fellow members that he had invented a far more powerful telescope than Newton's. He also told them that he had invented it five years before Newton's reflector, but could not pursue it because of the plague and fires that ravaged the country at that time. However, knowing that Newton's previous encounters with Hooke had led to confrontations, Oldenburg chose to hide this from Newton.

At first, Newton replied with conventional modesty:

"I was surprised to see so much care taken about securing an invention to mee, of which I have hitherto had so little value. And therefore since the R. Society is pleased to think it worth the patronizing, I must acknowledge it deserves much more of them for that, then of mee, who, had not the communication of it been desired, might have let it still remained in private as it hath already done some years,..."

A fortnight later he set modesty aside. Newton had changed his mind, and now wished to attend a meeting. In his second letter to Oldenburg, he wrote:

"I am purposing them, to be considered of & examined, an accompt of a Philosophicall discovery which induced me to the making of the said Telescope, & which I doubt not but will prove much more gratefull then the communication of that instrument, being in my Judgment the oddest if not the most considerable detection which hath hitherto been made in the operations of Nature."

Finally, Newton concluded the letter by asking "And by the way, what would his duties be, as Fellow of the Royal Society?"

Chapter 6:
The Three Laws of
Motion

"We are to admit no more causes of natural things than such as are both true and sufficient to explain their appearances."

- Isaac Newton

A Game that Leads to a Discovery

Newton did not go to London to appear before the Royal Society for three more years. However, he honored his word, and sent Oldenburg an account of his invention. In February of 1672, he wrote a long letter to Oldenburg and asked for it to be read aloud at an upcoming meeting. Within a fortnight, Oldenburg had the material typed, printed, and verified by fellow members of the society. He also kept his word, and attributed all credit to "the great scientist Isaac Newton, inventor of the reflecting telescope."

Meanwhile, the center Court at Trinity College was nearly complete. With a library, an atrium, a central fountain, and plenty of fresh grass to sit on, the place resonated with intellectual activity and enthusiasm. Students and scholars alike crossed paths there, and often spent their time discussing new ideas and discoveries, and the center reverberated with positivity. Newton and Barrow spent quite a lot of time there.

Newton occupied a chamber on the top floor of the building between the Great Gate and the Chapel. Occasionally, he stepped outside and watched his colleagues play a game of tennis on the court. Even when occupied with something as simple as watching a game of tennis, Newton's mind raced.

For instance, during one of the games, Newton noticed that the tennis ball curved in an upward and downward direction as it was struck the racket. He immediately understood the reason for the ball to spin in that way. He realized that when a ball is hit diagonally, it acquires spin. The side that is hit by the force of the racket acquires motion and acceleration. Newton understood this concept intuitively, as it was along the lines of a concept he was deliberating on for long (Newton wondered if light could acquire a similar spin and travel in the form of waves while pushing past air).

Newton was a gifted observer, but he did not take his assumptions for granted. When he observed the world, it was as if he had the power to peer into the underlying framework of reality. In an attempt to find answers, he looked deeply enough to untangle layers of superfluous content that otherwise distorted the truth.

He saw relationships between even apparently dissimilar concepts when no one else could. He perceived and understood the world like none other. When he saw a tennis ball spin across the court at Cambridge, he didn't see it as a mere ball hit from one corner of the court to the other. Instead, he saw it long enough and analyzed it deeply enough to understand the reason it moved as it did.

Lonely and dissocial as his world might seem, it was not altogether uninhabited. While most people communicate with other individuals, Newton communicated with forms, forces, and concepts unknown to others. In fact, it was he who unraveled, revealed, and propagated those concepts. One such concept eventually became known as Newton's Laws of Motion.

Newton's First Law of Motion

"An object at rest will remain at rest unless acted on by an unbalanced force. An object in motion continues in motion with the same speed and in the same direction unless acted upon by an unbalanced force."

In other words, Newton's first law states that objects have a tendency to remain in their current position and resist changes in their state of motion in any way. This tendency to remain in its current position is called inertia. Inertia is defined as the resistance of an object to change with respect to its state of motion.

The first law has two different concepts associated with it— one, which predicts the behavior of still objects, and the second, which predicts the behavior of moving objects. However, in order to understand these concepts logically, it's important that one understands the concepts of Galileo's inertia first.

Long before Galileo conceptualized the idea of inertia, people assumed that an external force such as a push was necessary to keep an object moving. For instance, people believed that when one pushes a table, the push is responsible for sustaining the speed at which the table moves. They therefore assumed that when one stopped pushing the table, it would stop moving too. However, Galileo looked at it differently. He believed that when one stopped pushing the table, the table continued to move along a certain distance without any assistance. He declared that it was friction (the force resisting the movement) that was responsible for stopping the table's movement.

Later on, Isaac Newton built on Galileo's concept of inertia, but added that the frictional force was dependent upon the mass of the objects. He stated that all objects resisted change in their state of motion, indicating that they are all in a state of inertia. Newton added that an object's tendency to resist change in its state depends upon its mass. He concluded that inertia too depends on the mass of the object, stating that the greater the mass of an object, the greater its tendency to resist changes in its state of motion.

Compare pushing a child on a swing to pushing an adult on that same swing. Given that an adult has greater mass than a child, it's safe to say that the adult's resistance towards change in motion (be it stationary or in motion) will be greater than that of the child.

Newton also stated that the force responsible for the change in motion must be unbalanced. To visualize this concept, picture a block of wood resting on a very smooth surface. Note that the surface is particularly smooth so as to ensure there is no resistance to the object moving on it. Newton's First Law states that the block of wood will remain in its current state of rest unless acted upon by an imbalanced force.

Factor all imbalanced forces that could potentially disturb the object's state of rest:

1. The first potential force is a force that acts vertically downwards, such as gravity.

2. The object is in contact with the surface of the table. Since Newton's law states that the force must be unbalanced, the second potential force must be equal in size to the gravitational force acting downwards. (At this point, there are two forces— the gravitational force and the force on the table, both of which are equal and are acting in opposite directions).

3. For an unbalanced force in the horizontal direction, picture a piston positioned horizontally close to one edge of the box. The force exerted by the piston becomes the third unbalanced force.

Assume that the three forces act on the object simultaneously. At this point, there are two equidistant and equivalent forces along with one horizontal force acting on the object. Driven by the frictional force— the push— the object will be set into motion in a horizontal direction.

So what caused it to move horizontally?

The gravitational force pressing downward against the block of wood is counteracted by the force projected upward by the table. Therefore, the two complement each other's frictional force, and neutralize the imbalance between them.

However, the third horizontal force has nothing counterbalancing it from the opposite direction. It is therefore safe to assume that the horizontal force exerted from the piston is unbalanced and is responsible for the change in motion of the object.

Picture a person jogging with a cup of coffee filled to the brim. Soon enough, the coffee inside the cup will spill. Newton's First Law attributes the spill to three specific moments:

1. When the cup was at rest and the person began jogging;

2. When the person abruptly halted his jog; and

3. When the person changed the direction of their movement

It is indicative that in all three situations the person changes the current motion (movement or stillness). Newton's First Law states that it is the resistance to this change (inertia) that actually causes the coffee to spill.

The examples do not stop there. From dusting a rug, riding a skateboard, and seatbelts, Newton's First Law plays a key role.

The law also made room for the discovery of concepts such as force. Through it, it is evident that all material bodies have a tendency to preserve their state of uniform rest or motion in a straight line. Therefore, in order to change the course of this path, one has to apply an external force on the surface of the object. Thus, the law defines force as an external variable that changes the state of uniform rest or motion of an object. In essence, Newton's First Law gave rise to revolutionary concepts such as gravity and relativity.

"The motions which the planets now have could not spring from any natural cause alone, but were impressed by an intelligent Agent."

Newton's Second Law of Motion

"The acceleration of an object as produced by a net force is directly proportional to the magnitude of the net force, in the same direction as the net force, and inversely proportional to the mass of the object."

Simply put, Newton's second law explores the extent of energy required to displace an object. According to this law, the path of the force acting on an object decides the speed at which it accelerates. Given that the mass of an object remains constant, increasing the force will increase its acceleration. Conversely, if force is kept constant, increasing the mass will decrease its acceleration.

Newton's Second Law can also be understood by the mathematical equation F = MA. Simply put, this translates to force equals mass times acceleration. So, in order to calculate the force exerted by an object, one has to simply multiply its mass by the acceleration. Similarly, in order to calculate the mass or acceleration of the object, apply the formula $A = F/M$ or $M = F/A$. In other words, simply divide force by mass to calculate its acceleration and divide force by acceleration to calculate its mass.

Contrary to popular belief, Newton's laws are not purely complex mathematical or astrophysical calculations reserved for intellectuals. They are practical concepts that are applicable to everyday life and are used by each and every person. They provide blueprints that address and resolve even the most mundane of daily activities.

One can find a number of daily life circumstances that function on the reasoning of the second law. For instance, most people recognize that a heavily-built car (such as an SUV) consumes more fuel than a smaller-sized car. However, many do not know the reason for this to be so. Newton's Second Law provides one.

To begin with, the mass of a heavily-built sports vehicle is much larger than that of a smaller-sized car. This implies that it will require greater force to accelerate it. Greater force requires greater energy, which is provided by the gasoline. Therefore, driving a smaller-sized car at 60mph on a freeway for 30 miles will consume less fuel than driving a heavily-built car at the same speed and for the same distance.

Similarly, the law can be applied to almost any moving body. Consider a man running a race with a friend several pounds lighter than he is. Although exercising the same amount of force as his friend, he has a greater chance of winning that race. As proved by Newton's Second Law, his friend stands a greater chance at winning simply because he is lighter in mass and hence accelerates at a greater rate. All other things equal, he will win the race. The only solution is greater effort to increase acceleration and balance the equation.

It is for this reason that most racing brands constantly look for ways to decrease the mass of their vehicles. The lower the mass, the higher the speed with which the vehicle accelerates. Likewise, the greater the mass, the more force, fuel, and energy the vehicle will need.

Newton's Third Law of Motion

"Every action has an equal and opposite reaction".

This means that in every interaction, there are always two equivalent forces at play on a given object. While the magnitude of the two forces remains equal, they always travel in opposite directions. They counterbalance each other, and neutralize any imbalance between them (as in the case of the gravitational and vertical forces explained in Newton's First Law).

Example 1:

Picture a person sitting on a chair. The person sitting on the chair exerts a downward force on the surface of the chair (as per the laws of gravity). Similarly, the chair exerts a reaction force that's equivalent in mass but is opposite in direction. As both of these forces interact, they counterbalance each other and ensure the person stays rooted to the spot.

Example 2:

A fish exerts force to push water backward by using its fins. In turn, an opposite force from the water pushes the fish forward. The same technique is replicated by swimmers. They use their arms to push water backwards, which in turn propels them forward. Thus, the action-reaction force derived from Newton's Third Law enables them to swim as effortlessly as they do.

Example 3:

A bird exerts force, pushing air downwards with its wings. Almost instantly, a reaction force is exerted by the air in an upward direction, enabling the bird to fly as it does. A similar technique is applied to fly planes and helicopters.

Example 4:

A car spins on its wheels and grips the road upon initial acceleration. The action force exerted by the car pushes backward against the road. In view of Newton's Third Law, a similar force is exerted by the road to push the car forward.

What the Laws Mean to Mankind

Experts in the field of science see Newton as the end point of a magnificent episode in human history, conventionally called the scientific revolution. His works, particularly his Laws of Motion, celebrate reason over unreason. It lays the framework to reason and examine the things that govern existence.

In addition to helping mankind construct and navigate airplanes, foresee car crashes, measure the mass of planetary bodies, and improve athletic abilities, Newton's laws are an accomplishment for humanity.

Although intellectual giants such as Galileo, Copernicus and Kepler created the foundation of Newton's works, their systems were purely mathematical and made little sense to the common man. Newton took the seed of their concepts, polished, developed, and broke them down into relatively simple statements that were not only more comprehensible, but also more applicable to human life.

Chapter 7:

Newton's Gravity

"This most beautiful system of the sun, planets and comets, could only proceed from the counsel and dominion of an intelligent and powerful Being."

- Isaac Newton

An Intellectual Epidemic

The scientific revolution that took place between 1550 and 1700 can be seen as an intellectual epidemic of sorts. Spreading across Europe for two centuries, it ended under the hands of Isaac Newton with his book titled Philosophia Naturalis Principia Mathematica, published in 1687.

When the world was still under the influence of philosophical giants such as Aristotle and Plato, the revolution saw the likes of heroes such as Copernicus, Galileo, Kepler, and Newton, to name a few, break norms and explore concepts that were never considered before.

Throughout history, scientists worldwide have seemed fascinated and intrigued by the world above. For centuries, people believed in Aristotle's geocentric view of the universe— that Earth was the center of all things. With this in mind, he claimed that the sun, the moon, and the other planets revolved around the earth. Although other Greek scientists such as Aristarchus and Samos rebuffed this concept and claimed that the sun is the center of the observable planetary bodies, their claims were rejected in favor of Aristotle's geocentric system. Rooted in the Aristotelian philosophy, scholars believed that the tiny bright objects spotted in the night sky were planets, and that they, along with the sun and the moon, moved around the earth.

In 1543, Nicolaus Copernicus published the revolutionary book De Revolutionibus Orbium Coelestium, translating to "On the Revolutions of the Heavenly Spheres." In it, he claimed that the earth is a planet that rotated on its own axis. He gave order to the other planets and described their motion. He also challenged Aristotle's geocentric system and put the sun at the center of the heavenly bodies. He defended his case by famously asking "For who would place this lamp of a very beautiful temple in another or better place than this, where from it can illuminate everything at the same time?"

Galileo Galilei used the newly-invented telescope to study the sky a little more closely. What he saw both encouraged and troubled him: he saw moon-like objects circling the planet Jupiter. He also noticed freckles and sparks marring the sun's otherwise bright and perfect face. He observed new stars that he never knew existed. He also noted the surface of the moon as not smooth, but rough and uneven. He believed it had mountains and valleys similar to Earth.

Johannes Kepler built on the observations of Galileo. With the help of Danish astronomer Tycho Brahe, he understood the orbits of the planets and discovered three laws to explain the motion of planets (also called Kepler's Laws of Planetary Motion). Kepler claimed that:

1. Planets move in elliptical orbits with the sun at its center.

2. The line between the sun and the planets curves out in equal areas at equal intervals of time.

3. The square of the period of the planet's orbit is proportional to the mean distance from the sun cubed.

Finally, to bring a fitting end to this spectacular era of scientific revolution, Isaac Newton improved upon the understanding provided and demonstrated by these philosophers. He explored and explained Galileo's observations of the rings around the planet Jupiter. Expanding upon Kepler's laws of planetary motion, Newton explained the motion of planets in definite terms. Using his laws, he attributed their motion to the force of attraction between planetary bodies and their individual masses. With this theory, he improved the fundamental understanding of the universe prevalent at that time. As a result, he derived something far more revolutionary— gravity.

"I began to think of gravity extending to the orb of the Moon ...& computed the force requisite to keep the Moon in her Orb with the force of gravity at the surface of the earth ... & found them answer pretty nearly. All this was in the two plague years of 1665–1666. For in those days I was in the prime of my age for invention & minded Mathematicks and Philosophy more than at any time since."

Back in 1666, in the gardens of Woolsthorpe, Newton spent most of his time contemplating his laws of motion and their relationship between planets and orbits. He gazed at the night sky and wondered what kept the stars apart. He looked at the ground and wondered what rooted it to its place. He also questioned that which made objects fall to the ground as they did. For the next twenty years, Newton wondered, calculated, and examined until he found the solution.

The manuscript titled Memoirs of Sir Isaac Newton's Life, written by William Stukeley, an archaeologist and one of Newton's first biographers, published in the year 1752, accounts the story of Newton's apple as told to Stukeley by Newton himself. In it, Stukeley conveys Newton's exact words as such:

"After dinner, the weather being warm, we went into the garden and drank thea, under the shade of some apple trees...he told me, he was just in the same situation, as when formerly, the notion of gravitation came into his mind. It was occasion'd by the fall of an apple, as he sat in contemplative mood. Why should that apple always descend perpendicularly to the ground, thought he to himself..."

As such, the apple incident was nothing but the event of a fruit falling to the ground. However, just as Newton deliberated about the mutual attraction that existed between all bodies both intra-terrestrial and extra-terrestrial, he watched the apple fall from its tree and began piecing together bits of the puzzle.

Newton understood that the apple was not the whole of the earth. He also understood that it did not represent the other planets. However, in view of the collective forces that make up the cosmos, Newton visualized the apple flying through space along with the rest of earth's contents.

Why, then, did it gently fall downward, instead of being flung outward? He had similar questions for the sun, moon, and stars: what pushed or pulled them away from planets?

"What is there in places almost empty of matter and whence is it that the sun and planets gravitate towards one another, without dense matter between them?" - Isaac Newton

Although Newton did not discover universal gravity in a flash of insights, (or the moment he saw the apple fall, as it is mostly misunderstood by people), these deep questions were the groundwork for a revolutionary discovery in the next two decades. While he might have first explored the concept of gravity in 1666, it took him twenty long years to share it with the world. It was only in 1687 that he spoke of his concepts on universal gravity in his book titled Philosophiæ Naturalis Principia Mathematica.

"What goes up must come down."

Newton's Universal Law of Gravitational Force

By themselves, the three laws of motion were revolutionary enough to take the scientific world by storm, but Newton didn't stop there. His mind was occupied by the influences of Copernicus, Galileo, and Kepler's heliocentric view and laws of planetary motions. He extended their concepts to a revelation that stumped the world. Newton discovered a law to explain the mechanics behind their motion (also called the law of universal gravity).

Newton's law of universal gravitation states that any two bodies in the universe attract each other with a force that is directly proportional to the product of their masses and inversely proportional to the square of the distance between them.

The Conception of Gravity

"Gravity may put the planets into motion, but without the divine Power, it could never put them into such a circulating motion as they have about the Sun; and therefore, for this as well as other reasons, I am compelled to ascribe the frame of this System to an intelligent Agent."

Gravitational force was the first force to be identified scientifically. To begin with, it was Newton's paradox; gravity both roots us to the ground and makes us fall. It explains how stars and planets form, and describes how they will eventually die. In classic Newtonian terms, gravity is the force that attracts everything that has mass to everything else that has mass.

The two masses can be anything, from the earth and the apple to the earth and the moon, or the earth and the sun. Newton's Law of Gravity helps explains why planets and orbits move around the solar system. Gravity demonstrates the mechanics of everything that moves— from tiny particles of matter and dust, to larger masses that make up planets and galaxies.

However, Newton believed that the strength of this attraction depends on the objects' masses and distance. He believed that the greater the mass an object has, the greater the gravitational force it exerts on the other object. As mentioned before, Newton also believed that the strength of this attraction depends on a second parameter— the distance between the two objects. Simply put, the farther apart the objects are, the lower the gravitational force between them.

The law can also be represented by the mathematical equation F= G m1m2/ r2, where:

F = Force of gravity

G = Newton's constant

M1 and M2 = Masses of the two objects

R = Distance between the two objects

This equation is important to predict the displacement between planets. For instance, it helps calculate the displacement of Neptune while predicting the displacement of Uranus. However, what the law doesn't explain is the mechanics of Mercury's orbit. While Newton explained the strength of gravity with great accuracy, he did not explain how and why gravity actually works.

"I have explained the phenomena of the heavens and of our sea by the force of gravity, but I have not yet assigned a cause to gravity."

It took another 200 years and Albert Einstein to predict that. Inspired, intrigued, and eager to look deeper into Newton's law of gravity, Einstein discovered the theory of relativity. He described gravity as not a property solely of mass, but a property of mass, space, and time.

There Are More Forces than One

In order to fully interpret Newton's Law, it's imperative to fully understand all the forces associated with it first. Newton's Law factors forces in a general way. However, in order to derive the ideal force power, one must be able to differentiate between different forces such as gravity, friction, and tension first.

For instance, the force responsible for automobiles to move is friction. When a vehicle moves, there is friction between the wheels and the ground. The wheels exert force on the ground as they spin. The ground in turn exerts a reactive force on the vehicle. Thus, the action-reaction force pair described in Newton's Third Law propels the vehicle forward.

Real-Life Applications of Newton's Law of Gravity

Newton's law is more useful to us than people think. In essence, it ties into almost everything in everyday life. The law provides the framework to rationalize even the minutest activities. It explains how things move or remain still. It demonstrates why basketball players are not flung into outer space when they leap into the air. It explains the way water flows and how buildings can fall down. With it, Newton's gave the world concepts to explore and understand everything that moves.

Chapter 8:

Newton and Alchemy

"About the times of the End, a body of men will be raised up who will turn their attention to the prophecies, and insist upon their literal interpretation, in the midst of much clamor and opposition."

\- Isaac Newton

A Golden Obsession

1936, Sotheby' House, England— amid a group of esteemed auctioneers, historians, and collectors, an enormous archive of Isaac Newton's private manuscripts was put up for auction. These records were deemed "not fit to print" soon after Newton's death, and hence were kept secret for more than two hundred years. It is in this year the famous economist John Maynard Keynes won the auction and acquired one hundred lots of Newton's hand-written journals.

For the next six years, Keynes poured through the records and worked to break the mysterious codes. What Keynes discovered both shocked and disturbed him. The documents drew Keynes into a world inhabited by people who believed in magic and mystery— the world of alchemy. He claimed that he had reason to believe that Britain's most famous scientist was also Britain's most knowledgeable alchemist.

Alchemy is an ancient practice that was surrounded in mystery and secrecy. In fact, for most of the early modern era, this practice was also forbidden. Rooted in a complex spiritual worldview, alchemists believed that everything that exists (metals in particular) has a connection with the universal spirit. It is believed that a select group of alchemists had access to the secret knowledge that they thought could transmute metal to gold. They believed that converting metals to gold would lead them deeper into the spiritual world.

Newton's journals have been made public in rare occasions since then, and they provide a glance into a time when the famous physician, mathematician, and philosopher may have forayed into a secret fourth practice—alchemy, considered by many the medieval forerunner for chemistry.

Back in the early 18th century, in his early sixties, Newton's devotion to philosophical matters grew deeper. Hailed as a revolutionary in his field and the author of the immensely popular Principia, Newton was a celebrated citizen. Yet despite the accolades and respect, he remained scarcely less isolated than before. He avoided public confrontation and only interacted with a very small set of people. At large, he was silent and isolated, and remained in his chamber for days, careless of meals and sleep.

Although records reveal that Newton showed glimpses of dabbling in alchemic practices during the late 17th century, his manuscripts reveal that he became particularly obsessed with the mysterious occult science only from his early sixties (in the early eighteenth century). It is believed that he feared diseases such as plague and pox, and often treated himself preventively by drinking a self-made elixir of turpentine, rosewater, olive oil, beeswax, and sack.

It is also believed that it was during this time that Newton became particularly curious about the study of chemicals and their effects on metals and human life. Some records claim that Newton believed he had the knowledge to convert metals into gold. Some claim that he wished to use his knowledge of science in this field to access a higher plane of existence. In fact, records also reveal that he was in constant contact with rather unsafe substances such as mercury, a chemical element so toxic that it is often compared to poison when inhaled in large quantities.

The followers of alchemy left behind a legacy of understanding the relationship between humanity and the cosmos. Alchemists lived in a realm that went beyond reason. They did not pursue proof, but blindly pursued that which was mysterious and, to some extent, baseless— a mindset that didn't mesh well with scholars such as Newton.

Back then, the modern distinction between chemistry and alchemy had not emerged. The literary world scorned their beliefs and viewed it as a fraudulent and occult practice. Back then, this discipline was largely unknown to society, and their claims were shrouded in mystery.

Partly due to the belief system of society, alchemists were often accused of witchcraft. In particular, the Royal Society considered it to be a dishonest and deceitful practice. People who were known to follow the practice were either condemned to death or sidelined for life. They simply disowned such people and ensured they had no role in the intellectual world.

Newton was a mechanist, mathematician, and a realist to his core. He belonged to the elite society that openly ridiculed alchemy. However, according to the records, it appears that Newton might have indeed been the most knowledgeable alchemist of his time. His personal notes (acquired at the auction) reveal another side to Newton; it appears that he might have met with mysterious men and copied their papers. A keen look at his journals seemingly indicate Newton's discovery of the philosopher's stone (a material believed to transform base metals into gold). In fact, his writings also reveal formulas and ingredients that suggest he was in pursuit of the highly coveted elixir of life (a substance that granted immortality).

"They who search after the Philosopher's Stone [are] by their own rules obliged to a strict and religious life."

Man of Science and Man of God

"He who thinks half-heartedly will not believe in God; but he who really thinks has to believe in God."

With alchemy, it appears that Newton embraced a world of mysterious fantasies— a world in which he could regard the invisible forces without having to see logic or purpose in them. Alchemy crossed paths with his beliefs on theology as well. To alchemists, the transmutation of metals was linked with spiritual ascension. They believed that it was God who breathed life into matter, especially metals. Soon enough, theology joined alchemy as Newton continued to search for knowledge that was known to the likes of God himself.

It combined with science to occupy the world of Newton's competent mind. When he was not lighting his furnaces or checking his chemicals, Newton was studying to quench his growing thirst for alchemical knowledge. By the start of the 18th century, he had with him a set of private journals that listed more than five thousand references to alchemic practices. These texts included formulae, procedures, and materials required to execute various tests and experiments.

Questions Galore

"Blind metaphysical necessity, which is certainly the same always and everywhere, could produce no variety of things. All that diversity of natural things which we find suited to different times and places could arise from nothing but the ideas and will of a Being, necessarily existing."

The manuscripts raised a host of questions that continue to intrigue many today. Was the founder of modern physics an alchemist? If so, what does it imply? Did he pursue his alchemic interests in pursuit of a higher science that was influenced by the idea of transforming base metals into gold? Did he interpret a secret theological meaning in alchemical texts that implied he was the chosen son of God (a common belief of alchemists at the time)? Or was he perhaps simply attracted to the science of primitive chemistry?

While no one can be certain that he practiced an occult science that was forbidden, there is enough evidence to indicate that his later years were spent pursuing a science that involved chemical substances— some toxic, some not, some metals, and some unknown.

It was only much later, when the age of reason grew more advanced, that the knowledge of substances was categorized into a specific study called chemistry. Today, that field is purely seen as a science that analyzes the elements of matter with logic and reasoning— nothing that's seen as remotely alchemic or occult.

Chapter 9:
Final Years

"To explain all nature is too difficult a task for any one man or even for any one age. Tis much better to do a little with certainty and leave the rest for others that come after you."

\- Isaac Newton

A Revolution in Science, Not a Best Seller

When the 17th century ended, the printed work of Isaac Newton amounted to little more than several hundred copies of the Principia. Apart from a few copies that were distributed around the continent, most of them was sold in England. Although very few people had the interest or knowledge to fully understand the contents of the book, it was revered by people as a sort of collectable. The fact that it was circulated in scarcity made them even more valuable. In 1713, a quarter of a century after the first book was published, its second edition was ready to be published at an expected cost of two guineas (nearly thrice the rate it was first sold for). Despite the exorbitant cost, there are claims that many students saved money for years in order to own a copy of the esteemed book.

Halley applauded the Principia. He declared that its author had "at length been prevailed upon to appear in Publick." Isaac Newton, the elusive and immensely isolated man, had indeed become a public figure. Halley sent a copy of the book to the King with a note, stating "If ever a book was so worthy of a Prince, this, wherein so many and so great discoveries concerning the constitution of the Visible World are made out, and put past dispute, must needs be grateful to your Majesty."

Halley also included a brief explanation of what the book offered. "The sole Principle," Halley explained, "is no other than that of Gravity, whereby in the Earth all Bodies have a tendency toward its Center." He added that Newton understood that the sun, moon, and planets all have a force that holds them in their place, and that he explained those very concepts in his book. Finally, he wrote about Newton's laws of motion and gravitation and explained their significance to humankind. Touched by this unexpected kind gesture, Newton acknowledged and thanked Halley for his support.

The Royal Society of Science Faces a Crisis

Meanwhile, the Royal Society of Science suffered financially. A decrease in members resulted in fewer contributions. Hooke remained social, and dominated the society with his views. Newton, on the contrary, mostly stayed away.

The world continued to be intrigued by numerical thinking. People sought calculations of all kinds to incorporate them into their respective fields. Mariners, architects, and gamblers depended on mathematical methods for their success. When one needed expert advice on the matter, Newton's name was above all others.

England Faces a Crisis

By the end of the century, England was poorly recuperating from the consequences of the war, and faced a financial crisis. Until the early 18th century, the silver penny had been the base unit of value. However, within a few years, gold joined silver and was exchanged in shillings, farthings, crowns, guineas. The newest and most expensive of them all, the guinea, was worth twenty shillings.

Unfortunately, their values fluctuated unpredictably, and this left people unsure of their financial worth. The result was chaos and disorder. No one was willing to spend their new coin in fear of it becoming irreplaceable. Instead, they hoarded or melted them down for export to France. The result was a shortage of coins in circulation. "Let one money pass throughout the king's dominion, and that let no man refuse," King Edgar said, urging citizens to circulate their currency more willingly.

Despite the king's demands, the melting houses and press rooms of the mint remained silent for long. Citizens continued to hold on to their coins and refused to circulate them openly.

Worried about the country's financial condition, the king called for guidance from eminent citizens. Out of them, John Locke (an English philosopher and physician), Christopher Wren (a highly esteemed English architect and historian), and Newton were considered. Wren was the first to propose a decimal system, but he was ignored. Instead, the chancellor, Charles Montague, knew Newton from Cambridge and proposed his name to the king. Soon, Newton was appointed Warden of the Mint.

Determined to make a positive change, Newton oversaw a radical change. Charcoal fires burned around the clock, and armed men and soldiers guarded the artisans during their work. Newton supervised the reprinting of smaller priced coins. He also ensured the higher denominations such as the guinea circulated substantially. The result was just as the king had desired, and British currency stabilized.

Among the Wealthy

The rich released a sigh of relief. As a token of recognition, Newton was appointed Master of the Mint, and earned a knighthood for his contribution by Queen Anne. With his new position, Newton grew rich himself. He received a monthly salary of £500 along with a percentage of every pound manufactured— amounts that grew larger over the years. Soon, Newton found a house in Jermyn Street. He also bought luxurious furniture and appointed several servants. By 1703, at the age of sixty, Newton was living the life of a highly successful and celebrated citizen.

His Quest for Alchemy Continues

Despite Newton's busy schedule, it appears that his alchemical furnaces continued to burn in secret. While the world saw a successful and more social Master of the Mint, once inside the walls of his chamber, Newton continued his quest for alchemical practices. He even worked long hours to make up for his busy schedule. He ate little, and often worked long past midnight. In his free time, he continued to write about the concepts that occupied his mind— thoughts about mathematics, physics, the mint, the Royal Society, and alchemy in particular. He wrote about his views on each of these topics with great purpose, perhaps with the intent of having it read when the time was right.

President of the Royal Society

That same year, Robert Hooke died, and Newton was elected President of the Royal Society. Having tasted success already, Newton happily accepted power and exercised it authoritatively. He also became more social, and attended almost every meeting. The withdrawn and quiet genius not only voiced his opinion on every paper published, but also asserted control over the selection of new members. In addition to taking things under control, Newton funded the society's depleting finances from his personal pocket.

The Great Man Receives Appreciation, but Remains Humble

Meanwhile, the world seemed to have changed around Newton. Gone were the days when men like Hooke waited to confront and reject Newton's every statement. Instead, people accepted and even understood Newton's style of integrating theories with mathematical experimentation. By 1713, seventy-year-old Newton was a familiar and highly respected name among philosophers. They readily accepted the very propositions that were rejected and scorned in the 1670's. Newton was whole-heartedly recognized as an inspiration for his contributions to science.

The Final Journey

Well into his seventies, Newton remained gentle and modest, and never boasted of his great feats. He also rarely laughed, and seemed mostly at peace with himself and his contributions.

In March of 1727, he died from a stone in his bladder, and never cried out, despite the doubtlessly agonizing pain wracking his body.

"He died early Sunday morning, March 19, 1727. On Thursday," the Royal Society noted in its journal, "the Chair being Vacant by the death of Sir Isaac Newton, there was no Meeting this Day."

Mortal Remains

He received full state honors at his funeral, and was buried in Westminster Abbey. Newton's final journey was attended by eminent figures from all over the world, each offering their respect to the country's notable and favored son. His coffin, adorned in crimson silk, lay at rest in the Jerusalem chamber— a room in what was formerly the abbot's house of Westminster Abbey— before it was placed in its grave. The procession was attended by most of Newton's companions from the Royal Society.

The chancellor, the Dukes, and the Earls were some of the eminent aristocrats who carried and followed Newton's mortal remains to its grave. It was, mildly put, a funeral fit for a king.

Condolences and Tributes Pour In

Poets wrote poems to mourn his death— "the philosopher of light," they called him. The nickname reflected Newton's contributions to the study of light itself, and is particularly relevant when considering that he is the one who identified and labeled the color spectrum.

In 1733, Richard Lovatt, an author and poet, published a poem in the Ladies Diary, an annual magazine that discussed science and important events. In it, he wrote:

"Mighty Newton the Foundation laid,
Of his Mysterious Art ...
Great Britain's sons will long his works pursue.
By curious Theorems he the Moon cou'd trace
And her true Motion give in every Place."

Edmond Halley's poem was initially written in Latin for the Principia. However, it was later translated to English and republished soon after Newton's death. The poem reads:

"Behold! You grasp the Science of the Pole,
Earth's wondrous Mass, how pois'd the mighty Whole,
Jove's Reckoning, the Laws, when first he made
All Things' Beginnings, by his Will obey'd,
Those the Creator as the World's Foundations laid.
The secret Chambers of the conquer'd Skies
Open to View. Hidden no longer lies
What binds the World's Frame, and the constant Force
Which rolls the farthest Planet in his Course.
Sol seated on the Throne commands that all
In Curves tendant to him shall ever fall,
Nor does he suffer the remoter Stars
Through the vast Void direct to urge their Cars."
England had found a new type of hero, one who
neither swung a sword nor spilt blood, but captured

the hearts and minds of people with his ideas and inventiveness. Many more poems followed.

Several years later, Theorist David Hume wrote that "Newton was the greatest and rarest genius that ever rose for the adornment and instruction of the species."

Alexander Pope, the great British poet, authored an epitaph that found more readers, writing, "Nature and Nature's laws lay hid in night; God said, Let Newton be! And all was light."

Samuel Bowden, a physician and poet, also expressed his views on the great scientist. In his poem, he wrote:

"Sages now trust to Fairy Scenes no more,
Nor venture farther, than they see the Shore:
They build on Sense, then reason from th' Effect,
On well establish'd Truths their Schemes erect;

By these some new Phaenomena explain;

And Light divine in ev'ry Process gain.

Such was the Path immortal Newton trod,

He form'd the wondrous Plan, and mark'd the
Road;

Led by this Clue he travel'd o'er the Sky,

And marshal'd all the shining Worlds on high,

Pursu'd the Comets, where they farthest run,

And brought them back obsequious to the Sun.

...

Mature in Thought, you Newton's Laws reduce

To nobler Ends, and more important Use.

You show, how heav'nly Orbs affect our Frame,

And raise, or sink by Turns the vital Flame:

How Moons alternate in their changing Sphere

Impress their Force, and agitate the Air;

How as without successive Tides advance,

While Cynthia pale pursues her silent Dance,

So does the refluent Blood her Influence know,

And Tides within roll high, or creep on slow."

James Thomson, a poet of Scottish origin best known for his book titled Rule! Britannia, dedicated a poem to Newton. Overwhelmed by the scientist' demise, Thomson wrote it weeks after Newton's death while teaching at the Watt's Academy. A few verses from his poem titled Sacred to the Memory of Sir Isaac Newton, read:

"Shall the great soul of Newton quit this earth,
To mingle with his stars; and every muse,
Astonish'd into silence, shun the weight
Of honours due to his illustrious name?
But what can man? - Even now the sons of light,
In strains high-warbled to seraphic lyre,
Hail his arrival on the coast of bliss.
Yet am not I deterr'd, though high the theme,
And sung to harps of angels, for with you,
Ethereal flames! ambitious, I aspire
In Nature's general symphony to join.
And what new wonders can ye show your guest!
Who, while on this dim spot, where mortals toil

Clouded in dust, from motion's simple laws,
Could trace the secret hand of Providence,
Wide-working through this universal frame.
Have ye not listen'd while he bound the suns
And planets to their spheres! th' unequal task
Of humankind till then. Oft had they roll'd
O'er erring man the year, and oft disgrac'd
The pride of schools, before their course was known
Full in its causes and effects to him,
All-piercing sage! who sat not down and dream'd
Romantic schemes, defended by the din
Of specious words, and tyranny of names;
But, bidding his amazing mind attend,
And with heroic patience years on years
Deep-searching, saw at last the system dawn,
And shine, of all his race, on him alone."

Yet He Left No Instructions

In eighty-four years, Newton had accumulated a considerable fortune— household furniture, crimson upholstery, thirty-nine silver medals, a vast library with nearly two thousand books , his many, many secret manuscripts, and some gold bars and coins.

Yet he left no will. With no wife, children, or anyone to call his own, most of it was distributed among his closest family members (his niece Catherine Barton in particular), some of it remains in possession of Britain's national trust.

Newton's Monument

Newton's monument stands to the north side of the entrance of the cemetery. His grave standing close to his monument reads:

"Hic depositum est, quod mortale fuit Isaaci Newtoni," in Latin. This, when translated to English, reads "Here lies that which was mortal of Isaac Newton."

Chapter 10:
A Legacy of Genius

"Religion and philosophy are to be preserved distinct. We are not to introduce divine revelations into philosophy, nor philosophical opinions into religion."

\- Isaac Newton

Newton's Laws are an Accomplishment for Humanity

The eighteenth century might well be regarded as Newton's era. He was modern science's favorite child, and his works continue to provide inspiration for many. With the Principia, Newton marked a permanent name in history. His views and beliefs marked a clear fork that separated science from philosophy. With this classification, people began to pursue them as two different professions respectively. Simply put, it created a paradigm shift and gave birth to modern science as it is known today.

Although intellectual giants such as Galileo, Copernicus, and Kepler created the foundation of Newton's works, their systems were purely mathematical and made little sense to laymen. With his characteristic simplicity, Newton bridged the gap that existed between the intellectuals and the common man.

For all of history up until that point, people believed in the myths that were passed on to them. With his simple laws, he shattered poorly-conceived systems and taught generations the truth that governs existence. He demonstrated to society by questioning and rationalizing that the human brain was capable of understanding concepts that were unknown to the world. His laws represent one of mankind's greatest achievements. They described the fundamental actions of nature with simple formulae, provided appealing physical theories, and laid the groundwork for many more theories to follow.

Newton's Laws Helped Humanity Understand Its Place in the Cosmos

For the first time in the history of modern science, Newton proved that the universe worked alongside the properties of invisible forces. He elaborated on Galileo's concepts of inertia, and explained that everything in this universe is resistant to changes in motion. He studied the laws of Johannes Kepler and Galileo, and charted and explained the planetary motions. With his research, he provided significant proof to support the heliocentric view of the universe. With his laws of motion, Newton further introduced concepts such as gravity and mass. With them, he explained why humanity both remains rooted to the ground and planets move. He described how planets are formed and how they will eventually die. In essence, he explained the course of heavenly bodies, introduced humanity to the cosmos, and helped it recognize its place in the universe.

Spaceflight Systems

Newton's laws form the basis for spaceflight systems. In fact, these laws reveal the secret for rocket propulsion in outer space. It is through his laws of motion and gravity that astronauts and engineers were able to make the giant leap to space travel.

Newton's Laws Inspire Future Theories

Not only did Newton inspire the scientific world for several centuries, he also gave rise to many future geniuses alike. While Newton was the first to introduce concepts such as gravity, Albert Einstein studied Newton's laws to formulate the theory of relativity. Inspired by Newton's work, Einstein observed that the speed of light in a vacuum affects the laws of motion. This theory set a new framework for physics in general. In fact, it introduced revolutionary concepts that govern the very principles of space and time as they are known today.

The Discovery of Calculus

Aside from his contributions to science, Newton had a huge impact in the field of mathematics. In fact, his studies in mathematics led to the discovery of modern calculus (a mathematical study that factors numbers with respect to their functions, limits, derivatives, and integrals). With this discovery, Newton helped mathematicians understand the behavior and rate at which variable quantities change. Using this discipline as the basis for further study, later generations have grown to understand the properties of motion, electricity, heat, light, and sound.

Every Century and Country Longs for a Son like Him

There has not been a scientist as revolutionary as Newton in the centuries after his death. Many believe that there simply cannot be anyone else like him. In the early nineteenth century, Georges Cuvier, a French naturalist and zoologist who is also referred to as the Father of paleontology, enviously asked, "Should not natural history also one day have its Newton?"

The 21st century continues to long for a Newton of its own.

Isaac Newton— inventor of the reflecting telescope, theorist of light and color, discoverer of calculus, developer of the three laws of motion, designer of the universal law of gravitational force, secret practitioner of early modern chemistry, and father of modern science— is by far the most influential scientist the world has ever seen.

Epilogue

"If I have seen further than others, it is by standing upon the shoulders of giants."

- **Isaac Newton**

There cannot be a discussion about modern science or scientists that does not include Newton. The man's extraordinary life and contributions to diverse disciplines can never be overstated.

His personal relationships were sadly few; he had a small number of friends and confidantes, and mainly kept to himself. Perhaps if he had been raised in a stable family environment this would not have been the case, and if he had had more people with whom he felt comfortable talking, discoveries like his telescope and the law of universal gravity may have been revealed to the world years sooner.

But in truth, Newton owed the world nothing. He had never been handed anything; all of his success, his discoveries, his eventual wealth, and his reputation were well-earned and hard-won. From a family of farmers, with neither a father nor substitute paternal figure who understood him, Newton had to scratch out everything for which he is known. When he passed, the world mourned, and for a man who had spent so much time in solitude, that is an exceedingly rare thing, and stands testament to his status as the first, and possibly last, of his kind.

Sources

Biography.com Editors. "Isaac Newton Biography." Bio.com. A&E Networks Television, 2016. Web.

Westfall, Richard S. Never at Rest: A Biography of Isaac Newton. Cambridge: Cambridge UP, 1980. Print.

"Isaac Newton, by James Gleick." EBooks.com. Vintage Publications, n.d.

Newton, Isaac, Alexandre Koyre[], and I. Bernard Cohen. Philosophiae Naturalis Principia Mathematica. Cambridge, MA: Harvard UP, 1972. Print.

"Isaac Newton Biography." Thefamouspeople.com." famous people, 2-16.

"Isaac Newton's Old School - Welcome." Isaac Newton's Old School - Welcome. Mrsite, June 2013. Web.

"Account of a Conversation between Newton and Conduitt." (Normalized Version). Editorship of Rob Iliffe and Scott Mandelbrote, 2008.

"'Qustiones Qudam Philosophi' ('Certain Philosophical Questions')." (Normalized Version). Editorship of Rob Iliffe and Scott Mandelbrote, 2008.

"Fitzwilliam Notebook." (Normalized Version). Fitzwilliam Museum, Cambridge, UK, n.d.

Janiak, Andrew. "Newton's Philosophy." Stanford University. Stanford University, 13 Oct. 2006.

"Isaac Newton Biography." Bio.com. A&E Networks Television, n.d. Web.
Helen Klus, Dr. "Newton's Theory of Light." Newton's Theory of Light. Arizona State University, 2013. Web.

Hall, A. Rupert, and A. D. C. Simpson. "An Account of the Royal Society's Newton Telescope". Notes and Records of the Royal Society of London 50.1 (1996): 1–11. Web.

"Newton's Reflectors." Amazing Space. Space Telescope Science, n.d. Web.

"Newton's First Law of Motion and Galileo's Concept of Inertia." Newton's First Law of Motion. Farside Teaching, n.d. Web.

"The Physics Classroom." The Physics Classroom. Tom Henderson, n.d. Web.

"Richard Fitzpatrick Professor of Physics The University of Texas at Austin." Home Page for Richard Fitzpatrick. Farside Teaching, n.d. Web.

"The Sotheby Sale." Welcome. University of Sussex, n.d. Web.

"Newton's Apple: The Real Story." CultureLab:. Amanda Gefter, Books & Arts Editor, 2010. Web.

"Optical Theories & Optical Correspondence." Welcome. University of Sussex, 2014. Web.

"The Portsmouth Papers." Welcome. University of Sussex, 2014. Web.

"Newton and Alchemy: The Chymistry of Isaac Newton Project." Newton and Alchemy: The Chymistry of Isaac Newton Project. Indiana University, 2010. Web.

"Isaac Newton-Answer to Everything." Bio.com. A&E Networks Television, n.d. Web.

O'Connor and E F Robertson. "Newton Poetry." MacTutor History of Mathematics, n.d. Web.

57082546R00109

Made in the USA
Lexington, KY
06 November 2016